Pill After Pill

G000229406

Jonathan Benjamin

chipmunkapublishing
the mental health publisher

All rights reserved, no part of this publication may be reproduced by any means, electronic, mechanical photocopying, documentary, film or in any other format without prior written permission of the publisher.

Published by
Chipmunkapublishing
PO Box 6872
Brentwood
Essex CM13 1ZT
United Kingdom

http://www.chipmunkapublishing.com

Copyright © Jonathan Benjamin 2012

Edited by Aleks Lech

ISBN 978-1-84991-738-4

Chipmunkapublishing gratefully acknowledge the support of Arts Council England.

Author Biography

Born in North London in 1987, Jonathan first began experiencing symptoms of schizoaffective disorder when he was 10. It was at this age when he started hearing a voice and the paranoia that he was being watched crept in.

Over the subsequent years, the voice began to torment him and he became increasingly depressed. He started to believe that cameras were following his every move and that there was little he could to do to stop the intrusion.

At the age of 16 he first saw his doctor regarding his low moods and escalating suicidal thoughts. Throughout the next five years he was put on numerous anti-depressants and saw various therapists but he remained silent about the schizophrenic symptoms of his illness. Jonathan feared the consequence if he revealed the extent of his inner turmoil.

Just a month before his 21st birthday he encountered a major breakdown which led him to being admitted to a psychiatric hospital and a diagnosis of schizoaffective disorder. It was here that Jonathan began writing poetry out of a difficulty in communicating his often violent thoughts. Writing his poems gave him a brief release from them.

After intensive therapy Jonathan was discharged from hospital and over the course of the next few months and years began to slowly improve. He eventually went back to finish his university degree in Manchester that he had left due to his illness.

Today he has made a recovery from schizoaffective disorder and is now passionate about reducing the stigma attached to mental illness, particularly schizophrenia, which is often associated with violent behaviour towards others. In reality, most schizophrenics are withdrawn and reclusive, as Jonathan highlights throughout his poems.

Contents

Pill After Pill

On arrival at Accident & Emergency

"I'm going to kill myself," I told the nurse.
"OK," she said, "We'll need some details first."

"I'm about to kill myself," I told the doctor as he sat by
the door.
After a glance at his notes, he asked, "Mr. Benjamin,
are you sure?"
"I'll prescribe some valium," he declared. "Call us first
thing."
"If you still feel unwell, we can try and get you in."

"But doctor I want to kill myself-"
I yelled, pleading for his help.
"-a good nights sleep," he said, "is all *you* need,
young man, to see you back to health."

Inject Some Happiness

Inject some happiness into my blood,
So it can swim to my brain and flood
Its cavities. Let it fill every cell
With its pure red joy, and cast a spell
To morph these tear-stained lips into a smile.
This content is the summer shower, to last a while;
It will cool and replenish the barren leaves,
But like my ecstasy it soon will leave,
And I am back in the afternoon heat.
I gasp for cool air, I burn in the sun,
I am back where I started, with the
Sadness in which I begun.

Jonathan Benjamin

Ode To Nina Simone

Nina, I understand you now;
Now I know what it's like to be down and out.
Now I've had that mood indigo,
And I've fallen so low.

Nina, I'm a sinnerman on the run;
Only your soul can save me;
At peace forever we will be one.

Nina, I know how you feel,
When you deal time away with solitaire.
When there's no place big enough for
Holding all the tears you're going to cry,

Nina I could lay me down and die.

Here Is A Man

Here is a man,
Told the Lord he hated Him;
Thus treads a path only fruitful of sin.
Bound to shackles; never, never to be released;
Walk seven thousand miles with no soles to his feet.

If every second more is spent here on his knees;
Lamenting and weeping, suffering and pleading;
Will the Lord forgive him
His schizophrantic sin?

Or is he doomed to drop unheeding,
With every new thought born bleeding,
And each new day to end his worst?
And will there never be any freedom? Not even in verse?

"NO"
Cries the Lord
From this pen with which I write.
Here is the man;
Scorned the Lord in spite.

Jonathan Benjamin

A Cry For Help

What do I have to do for you to see
This decay engulfing me?

Bawling on the train,
Tremoring through each limb,
A shirt that is bloodstained,
Still you don't see a thing.

If I hang from this tree,
If I drown in this lake,
Then perhaps you will see,
But it may be too late.

All Change Please

I want to be somebody else,
Anybody but myself.

The bus driver on my way to work,
The tailor that stitched his blue-check shirt,
The barber who trimmed his thin, greying fringe.
I want to be covered in his 'hammers' tattooed skin.

I want to have his wife, his kids, his home.
I want to smoke his reds, wear his spicy cologne.
If I could blend into the nirvana that's his life,
Mine would be a better one, sweet and ripe.

The air I breathe would be pure and untainted,
A wholesome man could be created,
If I could be the driver on the one four six;
A little old lady calls him Mick.

I want to be Mick and his rasping laugh,
I want to drink with him in his local, play him at darts.
Just to share one moment with this man,
Is better than any single element of who I am.

My existence is futile, escape my only hope;
If I believe it hard enough, perhaps my body will elope
And come to nest within Mick and his prestige-
Suddenly his voice booms, "ALL CHANGE PLEASE!"

I missed my stop.
A mile back I should have got off.
But I was entangled in a wonderful dream
Where I was made up of the perfect set of genes.

Where Jonathan Benjamin was a stranger to me,
And a bus driver's life I started to lead.
Now I run to catch the next one four six,
I ask myself how I escape from this:

Preying on the identity of everyone I meet.
The morning's action soon repeats,
As I hand this bus driver my eighty pence
And I regain this sickly sense

Of becoming a stranger whom only my eyes have met.
It's nothing complex;
Simply put, I'm discontent
With the person I was born to represent.

I just want to be somebody else.
Anybody but myself.

Melancholy

When the melancholy comes,
He pounds at my chest,
He rushes through my veins,
He smothers me in his caress.

Until I can breathe no longer.

Until my only vision is of death.

And until these thoughts begin to wander,

There will never be any rest.

I Took An Axe To The Sun

I took an axe to the sun,
Split it in two,
Rain bled from the wound,
Whilst the darkness grew.

I took an axe to the sun;
They say I'll be tried for treason.
I just wanted a moment's relief,
But now I've killed the seasons.

Survival Of The Fearless

Life is not about love,
Life is not about your career,
Life is about survival,
Surviving through your fear.

Monday's fear is mild,
Tuesday's fear takes hold,
By Wednesday I am crumbling,
And the doubt takes its toll.

The doubt to make dawn again,
To exist through this dread,
Every second spurns me,
To put my person to his bed.

But, alas, I have no courage,
I beat a coward's heart,
So I must keep surviving,
Till the fear tears me apart.

A Life In The Day Of

Put   On
A

H   e
a   c
p p y F a

Leave your depression at the door;
Fix your smile in its place.

My Cubicle

I'm sitting in my cubicle,
Back against the cold, stone wall.
I see a graffiti war,
Carved into the pastelled door.

The school bell rings,
A thousand footsteps scramble in.
I listen to the rain begin to pour,
The clamour down the corridors.

The bathroom stirs,
I wait for composure.
Now all that's left, a smell of bleach,
And me, glued to the plastic seat.

I should be in Maths,
But with my collapse the lesson caused a clash.

So I reach for the kitchen scissors in my bag,
On the tiled floor I place my blotted pad.
"I need to cut the label from my coat,"
I told the lunch lady, lump in my throat.
Across the shepherds pie they're passed,
"Watch your fingers," she said, "they're sharp."
I watch my fingers as they tremble and perspire.
I study my wrist, the veins run like wires.
And then I score the width with my blade;
A sudden rush engulfs my body like a wave.
I score again, harder, with pressure this time;
A release, as blood starts seeping through the line.
Once more, I slice the scissors across, faster;
As blood hits the cubicle, I cry with laughter.

My heart in my mouth, I slash my arms,
Till there's no more solid ground left to self-harm.

So what do I do now?
I can't go out and let them see,
The red dyeing the white of my sleeve.

I can't go on, adrenalines gone,
I should have dug that bit deeper when I was strong.

But what do I do now?

Sit and pray,
Wait for science.
Obscure my disarray,
Conceal the violence.

Wilderness

Walk into the wilderness
Barren is the place
Lay your head down upon it
Descend from grace.

Isn't it peaceful out here?
Can you feel the burden wane?
Do you see the darkness fleeing
Till a blazing light remains?

Well, then you are there
Then you reach a door
Turn the gilded handle
Hereafter is yours.

Today I Spoke With The President

Today I spoke with the President and he booked me a
room;
Crater Twelve, south side of the moon.

What to pack? I hear it's mild in June.
They're taking me away at 3 this afternoon.

I Am But A Shadow

I am but a shadow of my former self,
Since this cancer of the mind took over my health.
I sit each day in my white lilied cell;
Waiting with letters full of lines of farewell.

For this man has become a lost, little child;
Shedding tears for his Mother to soothe him with her
smile.
But no-one is coming. There's no sound but the
humming
Of the voices in my head. I wish I was dead.

How much more can you endure me to bear?
If you dispose of me now, I have everything prepared.
My will; a list of every single possession;
This is what madness time has done, hours and
depression.

Depression that's come to be my firm and faithful
friend;
The one thing of my existence I know I can contend
Will be with me until I am laid to rest,
And peace at last I can possess.

Until that day, I sit and wait.
The lilies start to wither and flake.
But I'm still here, a faded shape;
A shadow of my former state.

Jonathan Benjamin

Don't Come Into My Room

Don't come into my room;
Up Beelzebub's path,
On the carpet of broken glass.
The door's varnished in blood,
I've a Nightshade in bud.

Don't come into my room;
There's aroma of burning flesh,
A painting signed by death.
The ceilings crumbling in,
The wall's plastered in my skin.

Don't come into my room;
See this coffin for a bed,
Here's me lying in it,
A body coloured red.
A bruised, battered body;
A body with no head.

5,734 Prayers

When I was five, I drew a picture of God in class,
With a sky blue cloak, wizards hat, and mask.

Miss Ivy glanced over my shoulder, grabbed the
paper and yelled.
Oliver Robins asked "Is Jonny going to hell?"

In that second, the bell it rang and we packed our
bags to leave.
On the bus ride home I sat alone, crying into my
sleeve.

When I got in, I ran to my room, kneeled down and
prayed;
I begged God for mercy. I've begged Him to this day.

Five thousand, seven hundred and thirty four prayers.
Every night a new one prepared.

Five thousand, seven hundred and thirty four prayers.
Each one crafted with equal shame to bear.

Five thousand, seven hundred and thirty four prayers.
Were you even there?

Five thousand seven hundred and thirty four prayers.
I've no breath left to beg; I surrender to despair.

This Is The Last Poem I Shall Write

This is the last poem I shall write
Before my mind must turn to stone.
Just like every next page, it will be empty white,
With all but the darkness to bear alone.

This is the last poem I shall write.
There are simply no words left to say.
From here to eternity, and my last glimpse of light;
I surrender my mind to its fray.

Little Green Café

Just before I die,
I'll have a slice of pecan pie,
In the little green café off Bloomsbury Square.

I sit by the window, thousand yard stare,
And wonder what to do in my final hour?

The British museum has a lecture on the Cosmos
flower
At five. I think I'll have a look at the Rosetta Stone,
And a quick wander through Ancient Rome-

The waitress asks if I want my coffee "Black or
white?"
"Actually, tea please," I respond, *"I don't want to be
up all night!"*

She hurries away,
Laughing politely at the final words I'll say.
You'll find my spirit here, in the little green café.

Jonathan Benjamin

From The Edge Of Waterloo Bridge

Standing on the edge of Waterloo Bridge
With the cold wind cutting my face,
I glance down to the Thames far below;
It ebbs and flows, a sea of waste.

I hold tight to the iron bar,
Blades of ice begin to pour.
Behind me the sound of heavy traffic,
Big Ben strikes a quarter to four.

From here, heaven feels so close;
My madness dosed with urge.
London sits majestic in its sphere,
As my feet inch off the verge.

Then suddenly a voice behind me:
"Hi my name is Mike."
I pretend not to hear but he carries on,
"Please, mate..please don't take your life."

Mute, I turn to see Mike frown and say,
"I also went down this route."
Gazing at him, sorrow clouds his eyes,
This young man drenched in his Monday suit.

His voice is calm, mine sounds so weak;
As I speak, I begin to cry,
"i don't know what i'm doing anymore."
I was so certain I wanted to die.

But now looking into his placid eyes,
My reason seems in question.

He stands there soaked yet still bears a smile,
"Why take life to your depression?"

The rain has stopped and the dusk is drawing in.
"We could go for a coffee, talk it over?"
A police car draws up along the curb;
Mike holds out a hand, takes a step closer.

I take his hand, he holds mine tight,
"Life is about learning how to cope."
I climb over the railings, supported by Mike,
Around my shoulders he places his coat.

Three police charge out of their car,
"Are You Hurt?" "What's Your Name?"
A list of questions, to which none I reply;
Collapsing before them broken, lame.

An ambulance approaches into which I am laid,
Mike has faded from sight.
Comatosed to the paramedics surrounding me,
Their faces bleach to white.

When I regain my senses, I find myself here,
In a silent hospital ward.
With its white washed walls and smell of disinfected
air;
Here is where the suicidal ones must be stored.

Jonathan Benjamin

The Devil's In Me To Dwell

I speak in words unheard of by the ear,
And even to my own the sound is veered

To a corner where he sits; the master in my mind;
The man who controls every edge of me, serving his
time.

Master in my mind said he was an angel at first,
But later he confessed he was sent as a curse.

An offspring of Satan, a prologue to hell;
Life or death, *the devil's in me to dwell.*

Weeping Willow

The Willow stands central in the garden,
Weeping onto winter's bitter shoulder.
I hear her crying in the dead of night.
I pull a pillow over my head;
But the sadness still remains.

Her slumped trunk,
Her sagging skin,
A vertical eye forever open.
Her branches hang like broken arms,
Swaying limply in the wind.

When the morning comes I awake
With the same dread in my stomach
That she feels in her roots.
She wails ceaselessly.
The birds stay away.

Even a sleeting shower provides no relief.
She is forced to drink the rain
That prolongs her anguish
That adds another day to this persistence
Known as nature.

The poor Willow tree,
Baring her flesh for us all to view.
Wilting and whining at the oaks and beech
Standing tall with pride; something she never had;
Something she'll never know.

For she forever will weep,
Nothing can lift her weary head.
Let her pass on.
Let her century come to rest,
And fell her falling frame.

Pained Woman

She lies on thorns
Eyes heavy and worn
Trying so hard not to cry.
Her pain concealed and raw
She gathers all the strength she can draw
Trying so hard not to cry.
Her frame remains fixed
Her mind so firm to resist
Trying so hard not to cry.

Then down her cheek, a single tear slips,
Her composure begins to subside.
Like the last petal falling, you'll catch a glimpse,
Of a woman with pain on her side.

Jonathan Benjamin

Womb

If I could go back into my Mum's womb,
Assume the foetal position;
I would lie all day and listen to the rhythm
Of the sound of her pounding heartbeat.

If I could go back into my Mum's womb,
Roomed in the crib of her torso;
Wherever she'd go I would follow each stride,
Refuse my debut to the waiting world outside.

Pill After Pill

Pill after pill,
Still there was no change.

So they dispensed me to death,
Till all that was left:
A body; immune to all sense.

"I don't think I'm meant to be here,"
The only words left to string
While fingers clutched the trigger.

You'll see me at times,
One hand on the gun;
But too numb to take a shot.

Pill after pill,
Still I am here the same.

Recluse

I'm a recluse.
I'm Eleanor Rigby reborn.
I've had my use,
Now I'm being withdrawn.
Cut me out from society,
Forget me please Lord;
The only exit from anxiety,
Is to live with no accord.
I'm searching for a hole to nest,
Where light never goes,
Where my being is at best.
I've converted friends into foes,
Turned my family away,
Severed all ties;
I leave for St. Kilda Bay
Third Sunday of July.
All the lonely people, where do
They all belong?
How do the recluse get through
A life that is oh so long?
And when solitude is saved,
And my time is gone;
Father McKenzie will dig my grave,
Lay my headstone marked anon.

Qi Qi

Qi Qi was the last known surviving Baiji dolphin. The Baiji was a freshwater dolphin found in China until its extinction in 2002. This was primarily due to hunting for its flesh and skin.

She watched them perish,
One by one:
Father
Brother
Sister
Mother
Husband
Daughter
Son

Still every evening she would swim majestic
Toward the golden sun.

Jonathan Benjamin

Art Classroom

Ross sits in the art classroom
Painting by numbers.
Jason draws a landscape
With rolling clouds of thunder.

Tommy moulds clay for his house
Between his thumbs.
Jack varnishes a box
To give to his son.

Me, I sit with pen and paper,
Ready to write.
But all I have are these words
To speak of a plight.

The plight of these five men,
Each torn apart,
By the brutality of a journey
Disclosed in their art.

Broken men of each generation,
United in pain.
Forsaken by the path they walked,
Struggling to stand again.

Oh what creativity is born in this room
Out of such affliction:
Schizophrenia, Bipolar, OCD,
Depression and Addiction.

Broken men of each generation,
United in pain.
Forsaken by the path we've walked;
Resolute we'll stand again.

On leaving Bowden House

"Today is the first day of the rest of your life," the doctor said.

"But doctor," I replied, *"I'm already dead."*

Pill After Pill

Lightning Source UK Ltd.
Milton Keynes UK
UKOW05f2036140114

224638UK00001B/3/P